THE BIG, BAD COOK

Once upon a time, the big, bad wolf heard that the three little pigs were leaving their mother.

"Good," he said. "If she isn't watching over them,
I can catch them. Then I'll eat one for breakfast,
one for lunch, and one for dinner."

Wolf saw the first little pig in his house of straw.
He wanted that pig for his breakfast.

Wolf knocked at the door of the first little pig.
When the pig opened the door,
Wolf was not happy.

"Wait," growled Wolf. "This pig isn't fat enough
for a big breakfast. I'll make him fatter."
And his stomach went,
"Grizzle, grizzle, growl!!!"

Wolf went back to his house and cooked
seventy hamburgers and took them
to the pig in the house of straw.

"Eat these. I'll be back," he said.

Wolf saw the second little pig in her house of sticks. He wanted that pig for his lunch.

Wolf knocked at the door of the second little pig. When the pig opened the door, Wolf was not happy.

"Wait," growled Wolf. "This pig isn't fat enough for a big lunch. I'll make her fatter." And his stomach went, "Grizzle, grizzle, growl!!!"

Wolf went back to his house and cooked thirty-five cheese and pepperoni pizzas and took them to the pig in the house of sticks.

"Eat these. I'll be back," he said.

Wolf felt better when he saw the third little pig in his house of bricks.

"If this pig was clever enough to make his house of bricks, I'll bet he was clever enough to eat lots of food," said Wolf. "He'll be nice and fat. What a fine dinner he'll make!"

Wolf knocked at the door of the third little pig. When the pig opened the door, Wolf was not happy.

"Wait," growled Wolf. "This pig isn't fat enough for a big dinner. I'll make him fatter." And his stomach went, "Grizzle, grizzle, growl!!!"

Wolf went to his house and cooked sixteen cakes. He covered the cakes with lots of icing and sweet things and took them to the pig in the house of bricks.

"Eat these. I'll be back," he said.

14

For three days, he delivered lots of food to the pigs. On the fourth day, Wolf decided he had done enough cooking. It was time to eat. He set out for the house of straw.

He knocked on the door of the house of straw, but the first little pig was not there.

He knocked on the door of the house of sticks, but the second little pig was not there.

He knocked on the door of the house of bricks.
He knew the pigs were inside. He could
hear them talking.

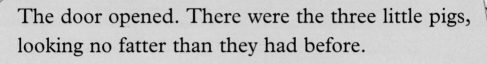

The door opened. There were the three little pigs, looking no fatter than they had before.

Wolf looked into the house.
There was a party going on.

Wolf saw a big sign that said,

**SURPRISE!
THE BIG, BAD WOLF
IS THE WORLD'S
BEST COOK!**

The pigs had shared all of Wolf's tasty food with their friends!

Wolf was so happy that he didn't eat anyone after all. He went back to his house and opened a restaurant.

Now everyone comes from all around to eat the good food of the BIG, BAD COOK.